CHAOS!

photographed  by Bob Gruen

D1604876

Omnibus Press

London / New York / Sydney

© 1990 Bob Gruen

This edition © 1990 Omnibus Press
(A Division of Book Sales Ltd)

ISBN: 0.7119.   Order No: OP 45798
Edited by Chris Charlesworth
Cover designed by Liz Nicholson

Book designed by Monica Chrysostomou

Artwork by Luke Wakeman

Exclusive distributors:

Book Sales Limited,
8/9 Frith Street,
London W1V 5TZ, UK.

Music Sales Corporation,
225 Park Avenue South,
New York, NY, 10003, USA.

Music Sales Pty Limited,
120 Rothschild Avenue,
Rosebery, NSW 2018, Australia.

To the Music Trade only:

Music Sales Limited,
8/9 Frith Street,
London W1V 5TZ, UK.

Printed by

Ebenezer Baylis & Son Limited, Worcester.

In the spring of 1976 my friend David Johansen came to my loft in Greenwich Village to visit. He was reading a copy of the English music magazine New Musical Express which I got in the mail because they often used my photos. Suddenly he laughed and said, "Listen to this review." It went something like this: "I went to a pub this week to see some new groups playing something called 'Punk Rock Music'. When I arrived the first band was on and was so bad and so loud I went to the bar for a beer and a double whisky. The people in the place were so weird and so rough looking I was nervous and ordered more drinks. By the time the second band came on stage I was getting drunk but they were worse than the first group so I had another drink. When the band I came to see, the Sex Pistols, came on stage I was so drunk I was in the toilet throwing up so I never saw them."

I couldn't believe this was really a review printed in a newspaper but David held it up to show me he wasn't kidding.

I said, "Sex Pistols is the name of a band? That sounds obscene!"

And he said, "Yeah! This is Malcolm McLaren's new group."

I met **Malcolm McLaren** in 1975 when he came to New York with clothes for the New York Dolls and he stayed to try and manage them. He was too late, though. The Dolls were falling apart from liquor and drugs. Malcolm managed to put three of them in hospitals and saved their lives, but he couldn't save the band. He had the idea to bring Sylvain of the Dolls to England and start a new group, and when he returned to England he brought Syl's amplifiers, guitar and piano with him. Malcolm started looking for musicians and soon found the would be Sex Pistols. Syl stayed in New York so Malcolm went ahead without him.

When I went to London for my first visit in the fall of **1976** Malcolm was the only person I knew to call up. I visited his clothes store called SEX and met Vivienne Westwood who designed most of the clothes. The store was on Kings Road and had a big sign in **soft plastic purple letters that said SEX.** It really stood out in drab, grey London. Sid Vicious was a clerk in the store then and he wasn't in the band. They had some pretty strange clothes. The strangest were leather masks with zippers over the mouth and eyes, and shirts and pants with straps to tie the arms and legs together. I had never seen anything like it and I couldn't believe people would wear them. Besides the weird stuff, they had some pretty cool rock'n'roll clothes and I got some nice hairy looking sweaters, leather pants, pointy Beatle boots and a leather jacket. Malcolm also gave me a Sex Pistols t-shirt which had pink and green pictures of a naked teenage boy! I couldn't bring myself to wear it. It was all too far out and strange.

That was just the beginning. At night Malcolm and Vivienne took me to a place called **Club Louise** to meet their friends. It used to be a lesbian bar so it was used to having a strange crowd. Now it was the first punk gathering place in London and I saw people in the most far out fashions and hairdos I have ever seen. One girl even had the sides of her head shaved and the top combed out like wings and in three colours no less! That first week at Club Louise I met Steve Jones, Paul Cook and Glen Matlock. Johnny Rotten was much talked about but he was at home with a sore throat.

I also met Siouxsie, Billy Idol, Mick Jones and Joe Strummer, Marco and many others. Talking and drinking with them I got to feel pretty comfortable and I thought they were all interesting. Most wanted to start rock bands (and many did).

I went to Paris for a week and when I got back to London Malcolm said I should meet Johnny Rotten and maybe I could do a photo session. I met him at Club Louise and he was the centre of attention, although it seemed that he had a negative attitude about everything. He wore a jacket with slogans written on it and with safety pins and even a syringe hanging off.

The next day we met at their rehearsal loft. It was off a street Malcolm said was Tin Pan Alley. Behind a building they had their own little two storey house with a rehearsal space downstairs and a loft room with couches upstairs.

Steve made tea as we waited for everyone to get there. I remember thinking that for a group with a reputation for being strange they seemed pretty normal to me.

I asked if we could start taking pictures in the rehearsal room. Since Johnny had just gotten over a sore throat I told

him he didn't have to sing because it was only for photos but when the band played he started singing. The first song was 'Substitute' by The Who (my favourite band then) and the Sex Pistols did a really good version.

I was impressed. I thought,

"They're not that weird... they're great!"

After a few more songs we went outside to take some group photos and Malcolm kept running to a pay phone on the corner. When we'd finished and were back in the loft having tea, Malcolm was back and announced that

EMI Records was ready to

sign the band to a recording contract. I went with them and took photos of the band with the EMI executives and everyone had champagne. A few days later Malcolm called me to Sussex Studio to see the band start recording their album.

I thought they were loud and rough but I like rock'n'roll that way. I thought they were good and they all had a funny sense of humour too, and I had a good time.

Malcolm with the group at the EMI offices in Manchester Square on October 8, 1976, the day they signed their short lived record contract.

The first time I shot the Sex Pistols was in London's Tin Pan Alley, Denmark Street, on October 6, 1976, on their way to a rehearsal in their studio there. They had a reputation in England of being strange but I remember thinking that they didn't seem that weird to me. I photographed them again afterwards, when it was dark, and these shots have been used all over the world.

At the rehearsal I was impressed at how well they could play. All that talk about how they couldn't play their instruments wasn't true at all. They played 'Substitute' by The Who and they were great.

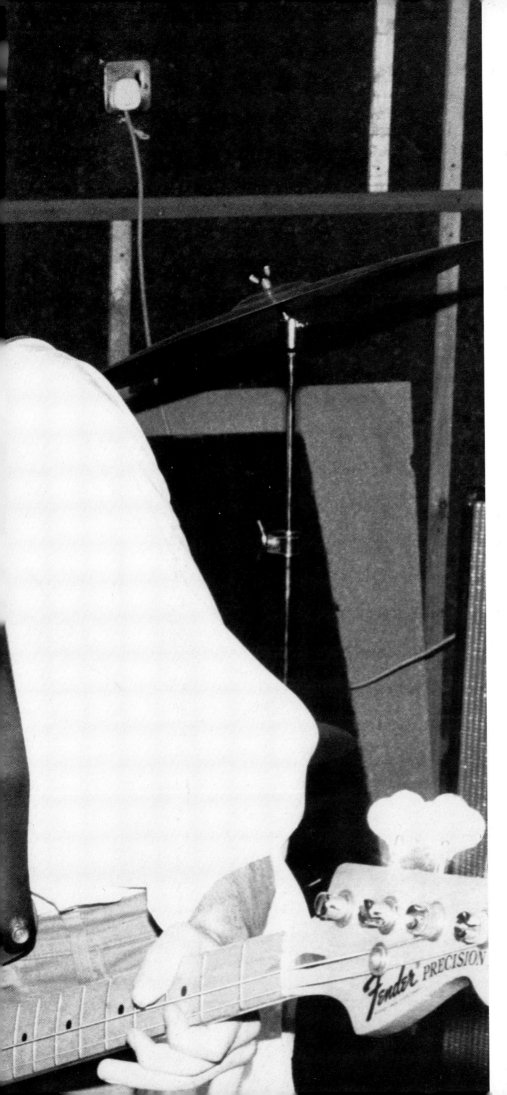

Glen Matlock, sharing the
microphone with John, only
had two strings on his
bass guitar.

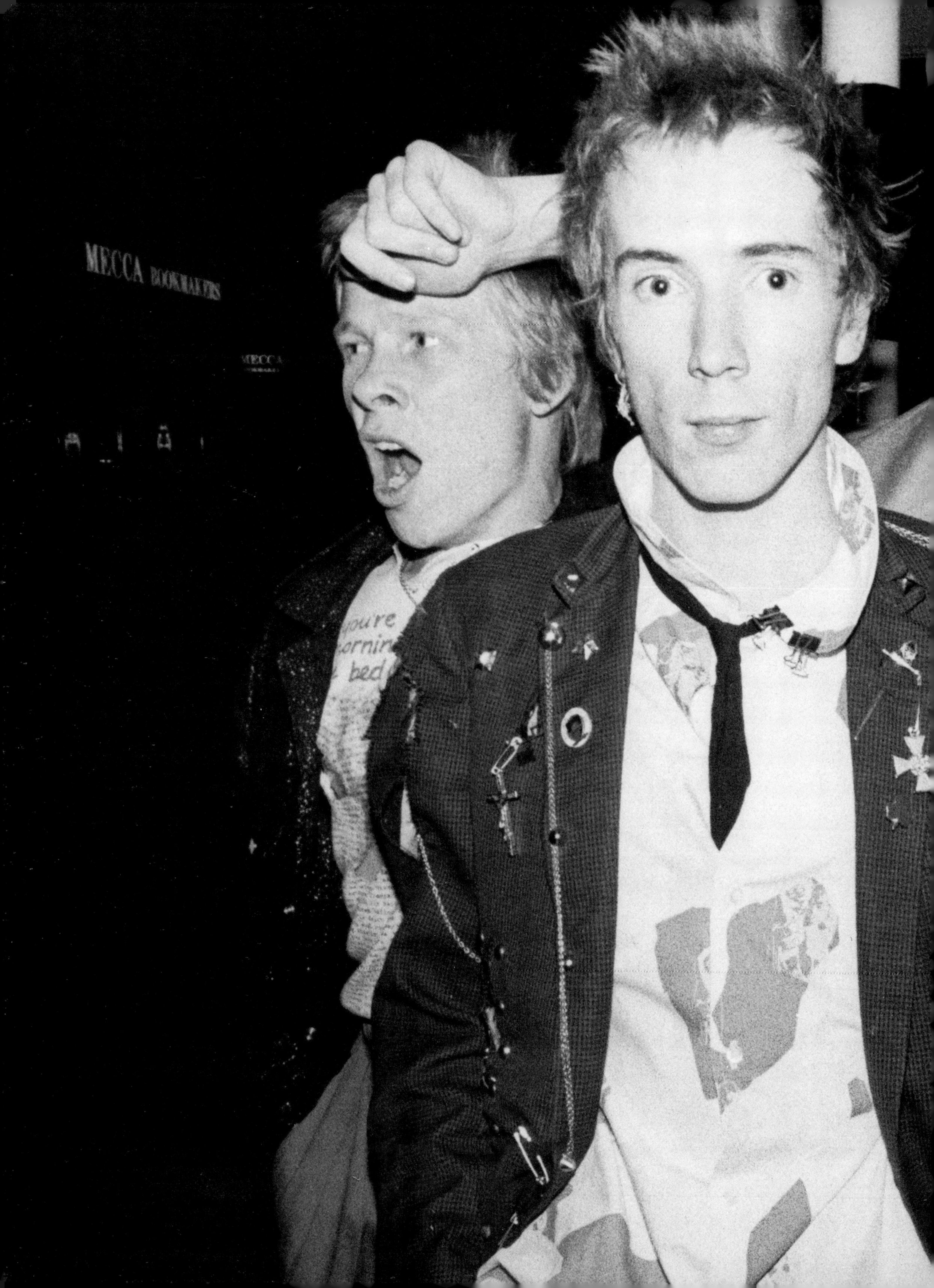
MECCA BOOKMAKERS
MECCA

7th October at the Club Louise, Johnny Rotten,
Steve Jones and their friends enjoy themselves.

Malcolm McLaren with the Pistols in their loft above the rehearsal space in Denmark Street. This was their home for a while before they signed with EMI.

After a night at the Club Louise, Caroline Coon, on the left in her pyjamas, invited Johnny, Sue Catwoman and Joe Strummer and others back to her house.

Simon, who helped with styling their clothes, Marco, Sue Catwoman and Sid hanging out at Malcolm's SEX store on Kings Road. Marco went on to play with Adam and The Ants and Bow Wow Wow.

Malcolm always seemed to be on the phone.

The official signing picture at EMI Records. Nick Mobbs, the A&R man responsible for bringing the Pistols to EMI, is on the far left. Other EMI execs are on the right.

John at EMI.

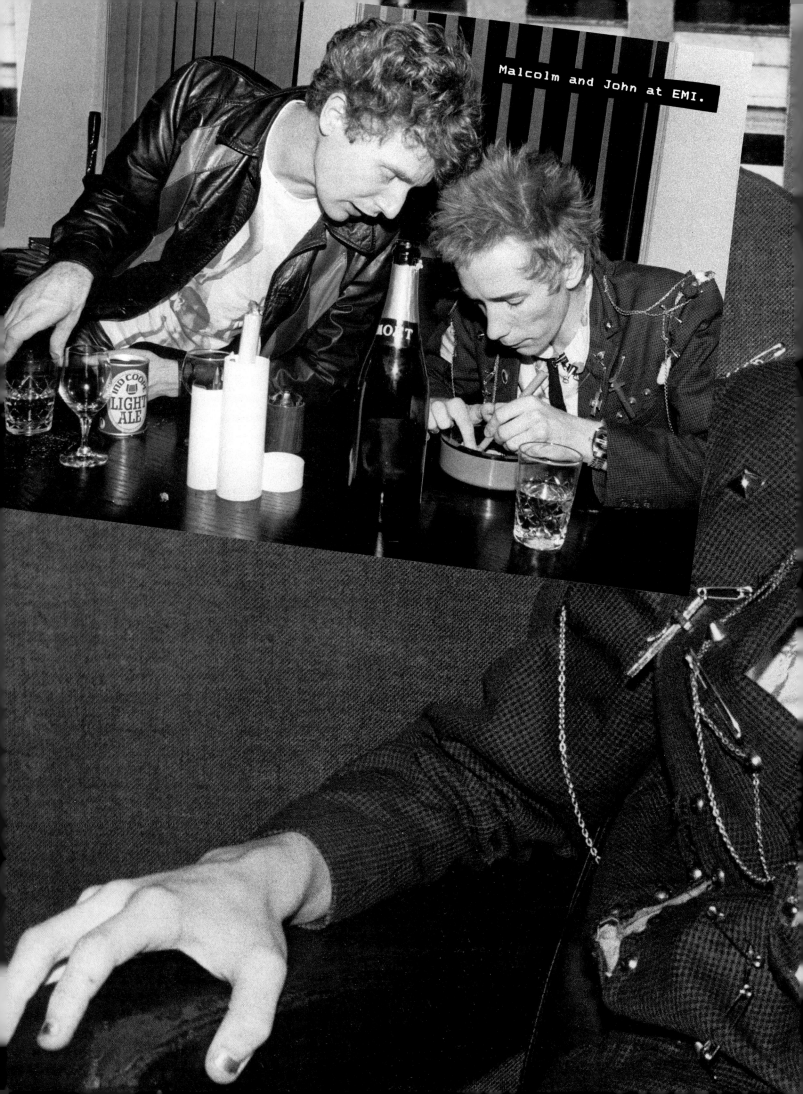

Malcolm and John at EMI.

Wessex Studios where the Pistols made their first recordings for their album.

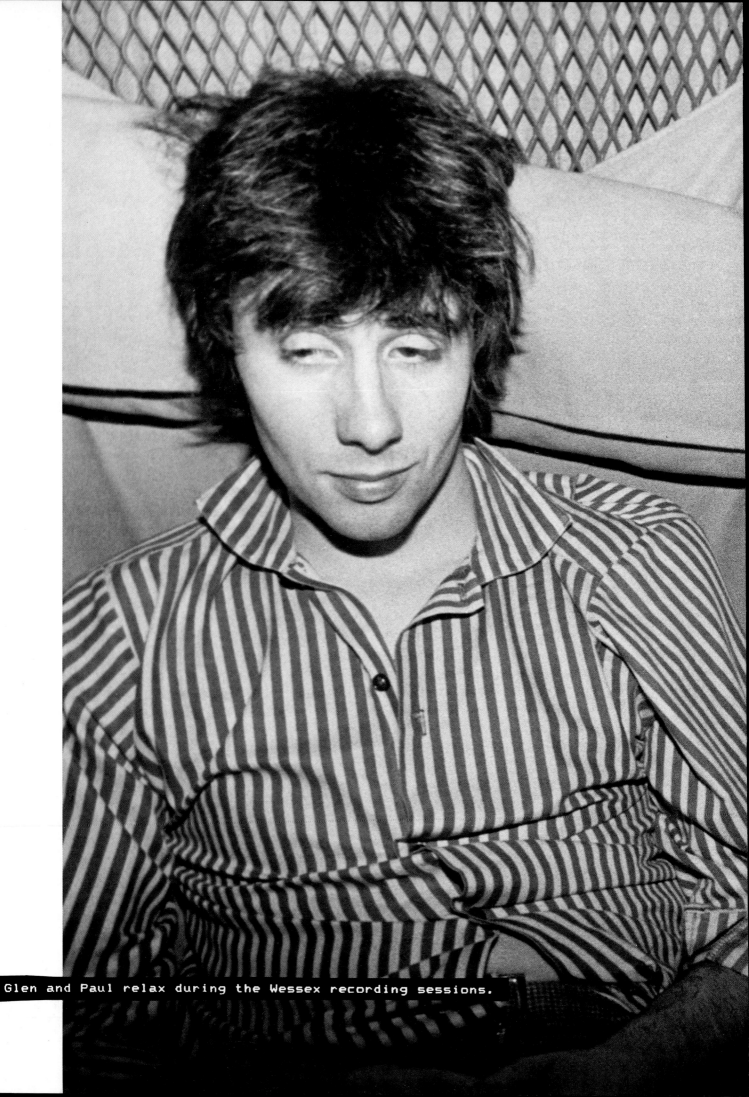

Glen and Paul relax during the Wessex recording sessions.

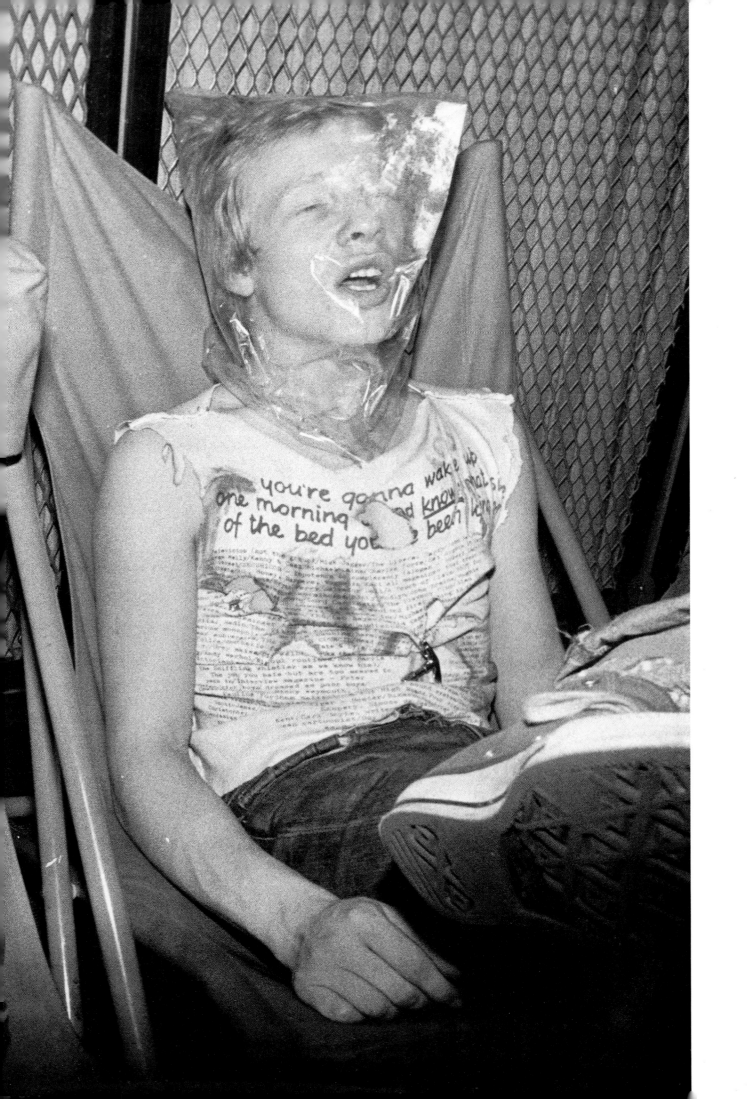

My next trip to England was in the fall of 1977 and Malcolm
had an office, the album had just come out, and the Pistols
were becoming very well known. The radio wouldn't play their
record because they said it insulted the Queen but that just
gave it more publicity and it was number one in sales.
Malcolm told me he'd try to set up a photo session with the
group and he gave me an album along with more weird t-shirts
(of Nazi swastikas and upside down crosses).
I played the record at my friend's house and it was so raw
and noisy I couldn't believe they had released it like
that. It was totally different from anything anybody else
had done.
Johnny Thunders and Jerry Nolan of the New York Dolls
had come to London to start The Heartbreakers, and their
friend Nancy Spungen had followed them there. I knew her from
New York. One night she called me and said her new
boyfriend, Sid, wanted to talk to me. He got on the phone
and said, "Oi! I hear you want to take pictures of me and my
group. If you want to do that you have to come here tonight
and lend me £80 or forget it." Johnny Thunders was there too
and I figured they wanted the money for dope. I didn't want
to pay for their drugs but Johnny and Nancy were friends and
I wanted to be on good terms with Sid so I went over, lent
him the money, and became Sid's friend. A week later, after
being scheduled on and off twice, I met the Sex Pistols
again and at 8 am we flew to Luxembourg so I could take photos
while they did an interview for Europe's biggest station,
Radio Luxembourg.
Everyone started drinking on the plane and when we were
met by a promo man he took us to a bar (where I shot one of

my best known photos of the Pistols) and then to lunch. By the time we got to the station everyone was pretty loose. Steve Jones dropped his pants for photos in front of the building and some secretaries saw him and the managers almost banned them before they started the interview. Finally they were allowed in and said some funny things I can't remember and the DJ thanked them a lot for coming. By the time we got back to the airport we were so drunk the airline officials wouldn't let us on the plane. The road manager had to argue for a long time and finally they let us on the plane to return to London.

Steve dropped his pants for this picture outside the Radio Luxemburg building, and as a result the group's interview was almost pulled off the air at the last minute. Sid's just behind Steve, and John's in the background with Tessa Watts from Virgin Records.

I flew with the group to Luxemburg on November 3, 1977. By this time
they were very famous, the leaders of the British punk movement,
and their reputation for behaving badly followed them everywhere.
It wasn't entirely undeserved.

Backstage at Winterland in San Francisco. Promoter Bill Graham had arranged for an artist to paint a Sex Pistols mural on the wall. Everyone was very surprised to see it.

In a bar in Luxemburg. The shot with the straws became very well known.

Two months later the Pistols came to America. On January 5 I went to Atlanta, Georgia, to see their first show of the tour. I was surprised at the number of reporters, photographers, and TV news crews there. They were playing in a small club for only about 300 people or so and it seemed about half of them were from the press. The place was packed when the Pistols came on. They played a loud fast set with **people spitting at them and throwing things at them.** A great opening show.

I had planned to go back to New York in the morning and hoped I could take some photos of the Pistols getting on their tour bus and then leaving. I woke up late though, and when I looked out at the parking lot the tour bus was already gone.

I was leaving the motel when I ran into Sid and the tour manager. They missed the bus because Sid had cut his arm badly during the night and the road manager had taken him to hospital. Sid said he asked one of the guards if his knife was sharp and to test it he ran it over his arm and he made a two inch long, one and a half inch deep cut into himself. The doctors at the hospital didn't get along with him and wouldn't stitch it or even put on a bandage. I went to the airport with them and changed my plans and we flew to Memphis together. I figured I'd see another show and then go home.

The soundcheck in Memphis was very good, probably the best time I ever saw them play. Everyone went back to the motel to rest before the show. When it was time to go back to the theatre, no-one could find Sid. The guards were running all over looking for him and were getting very upset.

Sid liked to show off the self made knife cut on his left arm.

They finally found him in the room of one of the editors of
    High Times magazine. And he looked high. Now the band
  and the guards were all very angry at him. At the theatre
      the crowd was restless from being kept waiting, and
some people had tried to get in without tickets and had broken

    down doors. There was a lot of tension and the show wasn't
      really very good. Later, back at the motel, the guards
  decided they would leave that night to escape the pressure
    of the press and the fans. I was saying goodbye in the
      parking lot, and Malcolm said, "Too bad you can't come
on the bus. We can only take 12 people and there are four in
      the band and two road managers and three guards and a
  secretary and me... well, that's only 11, so why don't you
hop on and come with us Bob?" I said "OK" and climbed aboard
                for a wild trip across America.
      In public the Pistols were **pretty obnoxious,**
but on the bus I found that they listened to reggae music and
were pretty calm. The next show was in San Antonio, Texas, but
  there was one day off first so we stopped in Austin to stay
  away from the press and the fans. It seemed that the record
company road manager had taken over control from Malcolm and
    tried to keep the band out of trouble. He had handcuffed
himself to Sid so he wouldn't wander off and Sid didn't seem
  to mind this new game. In Austin most of the guys went to a
  topless bar to see America and had a Mexican dinner and the
                next day we went to San Antonio.
      That night at the show at Randy's Rodeo the band really
    got things heated up. They taunted the audience, Johnny
  saying they liked all the beer cans being thrown at them and

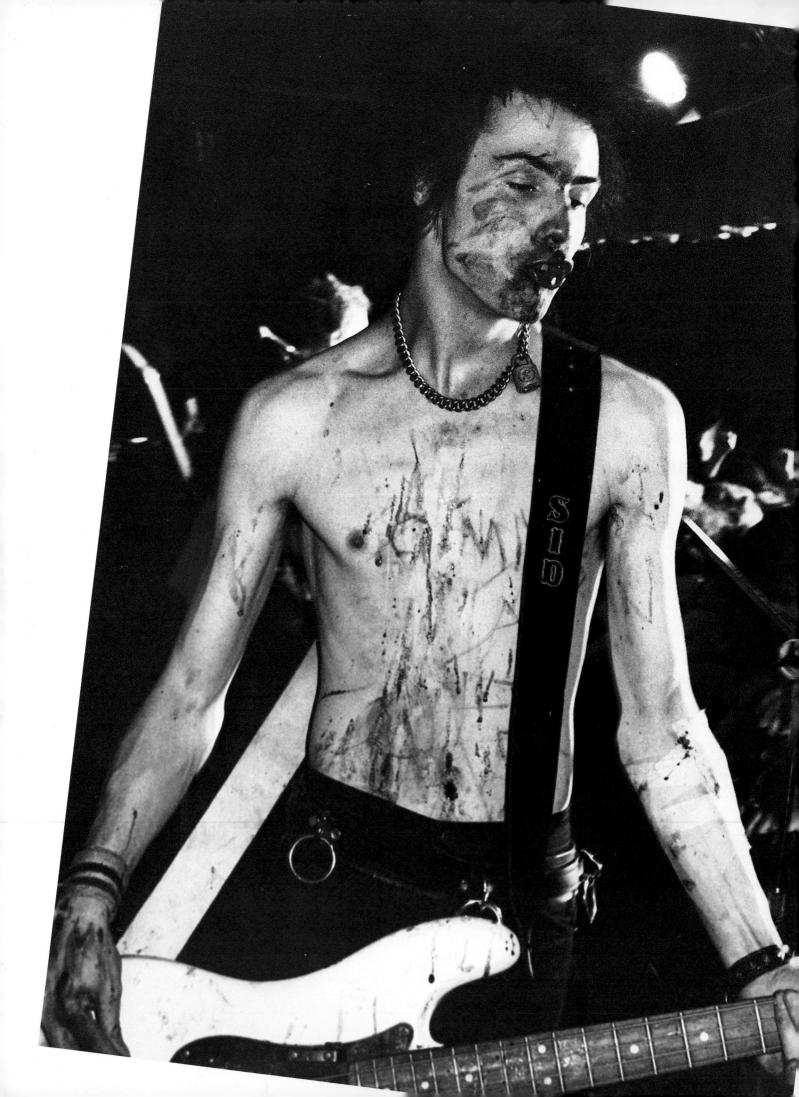

Sid called all the cowboys "faggots". A girl in the front row punched Sid and he got a bloody nose and started to spit the blood at her. He seemed to really enjoy it. When his nose dried up he took a bottle of beer from his amp and smashed the end off and scraped his chest to make more blood. The guard jumped out and took the bottle away and Sid looked sorry. He went back to playing and didn't even notice that when he broke the beer bottle he had turned his amp off.

The whole thing was CHAOS. Sid even hit someone in the audience with his bass. Later Steve and Paul were angry that he wasn't keeping up his part of the music and Johnny was angry at all the attention he was attracting. After the show lots of people came to the motel and the guards treated them pretty roughly, throwing them out and keeping them away. In the morning they found that several girls had spray painted slogans like "We're So Pretty Vacant" and "Anarchy In The USA" all over the tour bus.

We drove back to Baton Rouge for the next show and then to Dallas after that. The road manager was so nervous about the group mixing with people and making trouble that he started to change hotels so no-one would know where we were. He wouldn't even let the band off the bus at gas station restaurants to eat. Instead he would get a menu for the band to order from and he would bring the food back to the bus where they had to eat it. This kept things quiet but pretty boring. Travelling on the bus was a real contrast to the shows. Everyone was drinking beer (Sid drank peppermint schnapps) and listening to reggae music all day and talking. Then the door would open at the theatre and the press would descend, and the fans, and the band would be pretty obnoxious and the guards would be nervous. I thought it was pretty funny.

When we pulled up in Dallas, fans surrounded the bus. Johnny opened a window and a fan held up an album for an autograph and **Johnny spat on it.** The fan was thrilled.

We had a long drive from Dallas to Tulsa through five inches of snow and ice. Sid and I talked for a long time. He missed Nancy a lot. He asked me if it was true that in New York her job had been to beat bankers and other men in a brothel and I told him it was. It didn't seem to bother him. He said she was the only person he truly loved. He really wanted to get some drugs and to get high but the guards kept a close watch on him after he had slipped away in Memphis and he couldn't find any. Sometime in the night while the guards were asleep we pulled into a gas station where there was a restaurant. I went in with Sid and sat at the counter.

The manager ran in, very upset, and said "What are you doing?" "Eating," I said. "What's wrong with that?" So he left us alone and before I knew it Sid had started a conversation with a cowboy, his wife, and their child who were at a table. They invited him to sit with them and Sid carried his eggs to their table. After the cowboy heard that Sid's name was Vicious he started to challenge him and crushed his cigarette out in his own hand. Then he asked Sid what he could do. Sid just took his knife, cut his own hand and kept on eating as blood flowed on his eggs like ketchup.

The cowboy grabbed his family and ran out.

Sid really liked the engineer boots I was wearing and while I was sleeping he put them on. When I woke up he said he wanted to keep them and gave me his to wear. I didn't mind because my boots had been damaged and the metal toe was bent and it hurt my foot with every step. Sid said he liked them so we made a trade. I later heard that when I was

Here's Sid on the tour bus trying on new gear the band
bought while they were in San Francisco. My boots which Sid
took from me are on the seat to his right.

asleep he held a knife to my throat and told the others he would kill me to get my boots, but when no-one tried to stop him he put the knife away. After the show in Tulsa a bunch of people came back to my room to party. One was a big and beautiful blonde woman. All the local people were saying she was a man. Finally Sid said, "Am I going to suck your cock or your cunt?" She said "Cunt" in a very husky voice so Sid took her out to his room. He came back later said she had been a transexual and had scars around her crotch. We drove non-stop across the west in one day and got to Los Angeles at night. The band caused a sensation on Sunset Strip by stopping at a few bars and then we went to San Francisco. This was to be the biggest show of the tour, five thousand people at Winterland Theatre. Malcolm wanted to invite anyone in the audience to get on stage to be opening acts but the promoter wouldn't allow it. Before the show the band went to some radio stations and then to buy leather coats at a biker store. I saw the same boots Sid had taken from me and told him he could get a new pair but he insisted on buying me the new pair so he could keep the old ones.

The American roadies looked very different to the band.

Sid waits for food at a
truck stop counter between
Atlanta and Baton Rouge.
Just after this photo was
taken he met a redneck
with his wife and daughter,
and when the guy heard
Sid's name was Vicious
he put a cigarette out on
his hand and asked Sid if he
was as tough. When Sid cut
his own hand with a knife
and carried on eating as
blood flowed, the guy
split fast.

Sid and the Pistols' British tour manager Boogie, aka John Tiberi, wait at New Orleans airport after missing the tour bus. Boogie had to take Sid to hospital after he cut his arm with a fan's knife.

Americans check out Sid at New Orleans airport.

On stage at the Kingfish Club, Baton Rouge.

A TV crew greeted
the band when they
arrived at Tulsa,
Oklahoma.

Cains Ballroom, Tulsa.

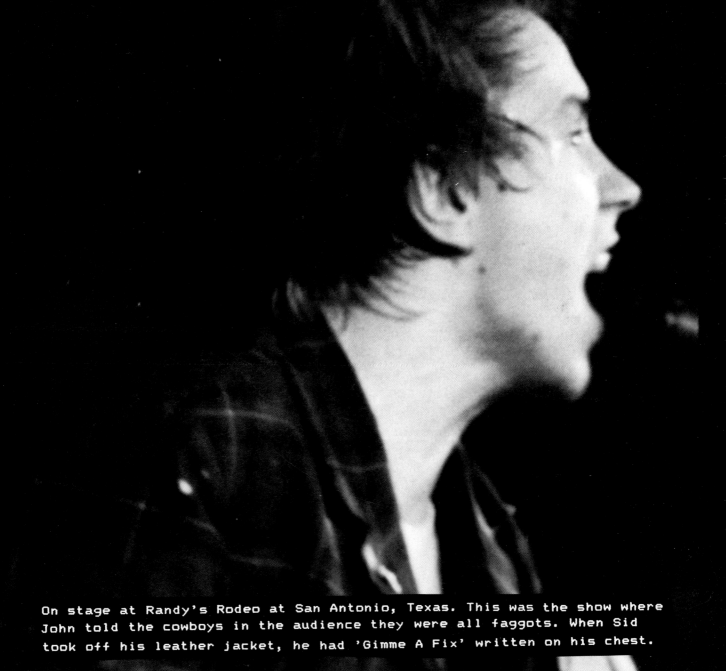

On stage at Randy's Rodeo at San Antonio, Texas. This was the show where John told the cowboys in the audience they were all faggots. When Sid took off his leather jacket, he had 'Gimme A Fix' written on his chest.

The blonde girl in the front row called to Sid and when he leaned over she punched him on the nose. He started to bleed profusely and seemed very happy. He later brought his friends backstage.

Sid with his new found
friends at Randy's Rodeo
in Texas. They had driven
from Los Angeles to see
The Sex Pistols.
The girl on the left
punched Sid while he was
on stage and a roadie
later threw them out of
their hotel. These two and
another friend spray
painted slogans all over
the Pistols' tour bus, much
to the driver's dismay.
I thought it was a
great improvement.

Sid gets to grips with a barre chord during the
soundcheck at the Longhorn Ballroom, Dallas.

John and Sid took part in a phone-in for Radio KSAN in San Francisco.

Johnny and Sid check out the seafood at San Francisco's Fisherman's Wharf.

Sid makes friends with a store guard in San Francisco while tour manager Noel Monk looks on. Noel sometimes hand-cuffed himself to Sid so Sid wouldn't wander off and get into trouble.

The Sex Pistols show at the Winterland Theatre was pandemonium. Thousands of people were yelling and throwing things at the band, and the band was yelling insults back. It was their first really big show and they seemed to be **well on their way to success.** After the show fans and press mobbed around them. Sid pulled some girls into the dressing room and then went off in a car with them. Malcolm talked of plans to go to Brazil to record. I took the first plane in the morning to New York and when I got home I started to develop and print my pictures. A blizzard hit and a foot and a half of snow fell. The next day Sid called at 6am and said he was in a hospital near the airport. He had overdosed on the plane to England and they took him off. He wanted me to come and get him so he could see New York, but because of the snow I couldn't get out to where he was. After two days in my darkroom I walked across town to CBGB to relax and there I saw Johnny Rotten at the bar. He asked if I had heard the news. I said, "What news?" and he said,

"The band broke up!"

Backstage after the concert at the San Francisco Winterland.
Sid invited the girls into the dressing room after they had
mobbed him on stage.

On stage at the Winterland, San Francisco, January 14.
This was to be the last ever Sex Pistols concert.

This Gibson guitar and Fender amplifier which Steve used
originally belonged to Sylvain Sylvain of the New York Dolls.